Mezzo-Soprano/Bel...
Book/Accompani...

MW01133461

THE
SINGERS
MUSICAL THEATRE
ANTHOLOGY

A collection of songs from the musical stage, categorized by voice type. The selections are presented in their authentic settings, excerpted from the original vocal scores.

Compiled and Edited by Richard Walters

ISBN-13: 978-1-4234-2370-6
ISBN-10: 1-4234-2370-4

HAL•LEONARD®
CORPORATION

7777 W. BLUEMOUND RD. P.O. BOX 13819 MILWAUKEE, WI 53213

For all works contained herein:
Unauthorized copying, arranging, adapting, recording or public performance is an infringement of copyright.
Infringers are liable under the law.

Visit Hal Leonard Online at
www.halleonard.com

Foreword
to the original edition

It is apparent to me that the most important and lasting body of performable American music for singers has come from the musical theatre and musical film. The classical tradition as it has been continued in the United States has produced few major composers who have written extensively for the voice, composing a relatively small body of sometimes profound and beautiful literature, but often relevant only to specialized audiences.

In pre-rock era popular traditions, the songs that were not written for the stage or film are largely inferior in quality to those written for Broadway and Hollywood (although there are plenty of exceptions to this general rule). Perhaps the reason is simply that the top talent was attracted and nurtured by those two venues, and inspired by the best performers. But it's also possible that writing for a character playing some sort of scene, no matter how thin the dramatic context (sometimes undetectable), has inherently produced better songs. Compare a Rodgers and Hart ballad from the 1930s (which are all from musicals) to just an average pop ballad from that time not from the stage or screen, if you can dig one up, and you might see what I mean. Popular music of the rock era, primarily performers writing dance music for themselves to record, is almost a completely different aesthetic, and is most often ungratifying for the average singer to present in a typical performance with piano accompaniment.

The five volumes that comprise the original edition of *The Singer's Musical Theatre Anthology*, released in 1986, contain many of the most famous songs for a voice type, as well as being peppered with some more unusual choices. Volume Two of the series allows a deeper investigation into the available literature. This revised edition (2000) adds some significant songs. I have attempted to include a wide range of music, appealing to many different tastes and musical and vocal needs. As in the first volumes, whenever possible the songs are presented in what is their most authentic setting, excerpted from the vocal score or piano/rehearsal score, in the key originally performed and with the original piano accompaniment arrangement (which is really a representation of the orchestra, of course, although Kurt Weill was practically the only Broadway composer to orchestrate his own shows). A student of this subject will notice that these accompaniments are quite a bit different from the standard sheet music arrangements that were published of many of these songs, where the melody is put into a simplified piano part and moved into a convenient and easy piano key, without much regard to vocal range.

In the mezzo-soprano/belter volumes, I have restricted the choices to songs for a belting range, although they don't necessarily need to be belted, and put any songs sung in what theatre people call "head voice" or "soprano voice" in the soprano volumes. Classically trained mezzo-sopranos will be comfortable with many of the songs in the soprano books.

The "original" keys are presented here, although that often means only the most comfortable key for the original performer. Transpositions for this music are perfectly acceptable. Some songs in these volumes might be successfully sung by any voice type. Classical singers and teachers using these books should remember that the soprano tessitura of this style of material, which often seems very low, was a deliberate aesthetic choice, aimed at clarity of diction, often done to avoid a cultured sound in a singing voice inappropriate to the desired character of the song and role, keeping what I term a Broadway ingenue range. Barbara Cook and Julie Andrews are famous examples of this kind of soprano, with singing concentrated in an expressive and strong middle voice.

Richard Walters, editor
May, 2000

THE SINGER'S MUSICAL THEATRE ANTHOLOGY

Mezzo-Soprano/Belter Volume 2

Contents

Pianists on the CDs: [1] Brian Dean [2] Ruben Piirainen [3] Christopher Ruck [4] Richard Walters

ABOUT THE SHOWS

ALLEGRO

MUSIC: Richard Rodgers
LYRICS AND BOOK: Oscar Hammerstein II
DIRECTOR AND CHOREOGRAPHER: Agnes de Mille
OPENED: 10/10/47, New York; a run of 315 performances

The third Rodgers and Hammerstein Broadway musical, *Allegro* was their first with a story that had not been based on a previous source. It was a particularly ambitious undertaking, with a theme dealing with the corrupting effect of big institutions on the young and idealistic. The saga is told through the life of a doctor, Joseph Taylor Jr., from his birth in a small midwestern town to his 35th year. We follow Joe's progress as he grows up, goes to school, marries a local belle, joins the staff of a large Chicago hospital that panders to wealthy hypochondriacs, discovers that his wife is unfaithful, and, in the end, returns to his home town with his adoring nurse, Emily, to rededicate his life to healing the sick and helping the needy. The show's innovations included a Greek chorus to comment on the action both to the actors and the audience, and the use of multi-level performaing areas with abstract sets. "The Gentleman Is a Dope" is sung by Emily about Joe near the end of the show, just before they declare their affection for one another.

ANYONE CAN WHISTLE

MUSIC AND LYRICS: Stephen Sondheim
BOOK: Arthur Laurents
DIRECTOR: Arthur Laurents
CHOREOGRAPHER: Herbert Ross
OPENED: 4/4/64, New York; a run of 9 performances

Something of a "cult" musical, *Anyone Can Whistle* is an allegorical satire about a corrupt mayor of a bankrupt town who comes up with a scheme to attract tourists: a fake miracle in which a stream of water appears to spout out of a solid rock. The town soon becomes a mecca for the gullible and the pious, but the hoax is exposed when the inmates of a mental institution called the Cookie Jar get mixed up with the pilgrims. Fay is the head nurse at the Cookie Jar, so inhibited that she can't whistle. She sings "There Won't Be Trumpets" about an expectant hero to rescue both her and the situation. The song was cut from the show while on the road and wasn't heard on Broadway. The New York run featured Angela Lansbury in her first Broadway musical, Lee Remick and Harry Guardino.

ANYTHING GOES

MUSIC AND LYRICS: Cole Porter
BOOK: Guy Bolton & P.G. Wodehouse, Howard Lindsay & Russel Crouse
DIRECTOR: Howard Lindsay
CHOREOGRAPHER: Robert Alton
OPENED: 11/21/34, New York; a run of 420 performances

Cole Porter's best score of the 1930s is a fun-filled story taking place on an ocean liner about a group of oddball characters, including a nightclub singer, an enamoured stow away, a debutante, and an underworld criminal disguised as a clergyman. Featuring a fresh, young Ethel Merman, the show was one of the biggest hits of its time, containing such hits as the title song, "You're the Top," "I Get a Kick Out of You," "Blow, Gabriel, Blow," and "All Through the Night." *Anything Goes* played Off Broadway in a 1962 production (239 performances), and enjoyed its biggest success in a 1987 Broadway revival starring Patti LuPone (804 performances). There is a 1936 filmed version, and another movie from 1956 with the title *Anything Goes*, but which bears little resemblance to the original. An excellent new recording, faithful to the 1934 original production, was released in the 1980s featuring Frederica Von Stade, Cris Groenendaal, and Kim Criswell.

The material in this section is by Stanley Green, Richard Walters, and Robert Viagas, some of which was previously published elsewhere.

BABES IN ARMS

MUSIC: Richard Rodgers
LYRICS: Lorenz Hart
BOOK: Richard Rodgers and Lorenz Hart
DIRECTOR: Robert Sinclair
CHOREOGRAPHER: George Balanchine
OPENED: 4/14/37, New York; a run of 289 performances

With such songs as "I Wish I Were in Love Again," "Johnny One Note," "The Lady Is a Tramp," "My Funny Valentine," and "Where or When," *Babes in Arms* could claim more hits than any other Rodgers and Hart musical. In the high-spirited, youthful show, a group of teenagers, whose parents are out-of-work vaudevillians, stage a revue to keep from being sent to a work farm. Unfortunately, the show is a bomb. Later, when a transatlantic French flyer lands nearby, they are able to attract enough publicity to put on a successful show and build their own youth center. Because the sets were modest and the cast boasted no stellar names, producer Dwight Deere Wiman priced his tickets at a bargain $3.85 top. In 1959 the plot of the show was revised, the characters names were changed, and the song list slightly altered. (There was never much plot anyway.) The 1939 movie version featured Judy Garland and Mickey Rooney.

BALLROOM

MUSIC: Billy Goldenberg
LYRICS: Alan and Marilyn Bergman
BOOK: Jerome Kass
DIRECTOR AND CHOREOGRAPHER: Michael Bennett
OPENED: 3/24/79, New York; a run of 116 performances

Ballroom, an extravagant Michael Bennett production, was one of the most expensive productions ever to reach Broadway, highly fanfared before its New York opening, then closed after a very brief run. The spirit of the show rode on the nostalgia wave of the 1970s. "Fifty Percent" was the show's standout song, and has become a standard of sorts in theatre circles.

BELLS ARE RINGING

MUSIC: Jule Styne
BOOK AND LYRICS: Betty Comden and Adolph Green
DIRECTOR: Jerome Robbins
CHOREOGRAPHERS: Jerome Robbins and Bob Fosse
OPENED: 11/29/56, New York; a run of 924 performances

Ever since appearing together in a nightclub revue, Betty Comden and Adolph Green had wanted to write a musical for their friend, Judy Holliday. The idea they eventually hit upon was to cast Miss Holliday as a meddlesome operator at a telephone answering service who gets involved with her clients' lives. She is in fact so helpful to one, a playwright in need of inspiration, that they meet, fall in love—though through it all she conceals her true identity—dance and sing in the subway, and entertain fellow New Yorkers in Central Park. At last she confesses that she's the operator, and they go off to loveland. "The Party's Over" is sung when she realizes she has to tell Jeff who she is, and she believes he'll dump her. A film version was made that is virtually the stage show on film, with Dean Martin playing opposite Miss Holliday.

CHESS

MUSIC: Benny Andersson and Bjorn Ulvaeus
LYRICS: Tim Rice
BOOK: Richard Nelson, based on an idea by Tim Rice
DIRECTOR: Trevor Nunn
CHOREOGRAPHER: Lynne Taylor-Corbett
OPENED: 4/28/88, New York; a run of 68 performances

There have been musicals about the cold war (*Leave It to Me!*, *Silk Stockings*), but *Chess* was the first to treat the conflict seriously, using an international chess match as a metaphor. The idea originated with Tim Rice who first tried to interest his former partner, Andrew Lloyd Webber, in the project. When that failed, he approached Andersson and Ulvaeus, writers and singers with the Swedish pop group ABBA. Like *Jesus Christ Superstar* and *Evita, Chess* originated as a successful record album before it became a stage production. Trevor Nunn took over directing the show when Michael Bennett withdrew because of illness. The London production was a high tech spectacle, rock opera type presentation. The libretto was revised for New York, and a different production approach was tried. "Someone Else's Story" was added for the Broadway run. The story is a romantic triangle with a Bobby Fischer type American chess champion, a Russian opponent who defects to the West, and the Hungarian born American woman who transfers her affections from the American to the Russian without bringing happiness to anyone. Though the show ran three years in London, it never made back its initial investment there. It lost $6,000,000 in New York.

A CHORUS LINE

MUSIC: Marvin Hamlisch
LYRICS: Edward Kleban
BOOK: James Kirkwood and Nicholas Dante
DIRECTOR AND CHOREOGRAPHER: Michael Bennett
OPENED: 7/25/75, New York; a run of 6,137 performances

Beginning with the deceptively simple premise of an audition for chorus dancers, *A Chorus Line* eventually proves to be an interesting examination of the dancer's thoughts and feelings, shown in monologues, dialogues, solo songs, and ensembles. Created as a workshop production in Joseph Papp's Public Theatre, the show, like *Company* and *Follies* before it, has no traditional plot, and has been widely imitated. *A Chorus Line* had one of the longest running productions in Broadway history with a run of 15 years.

COMPANY

MUSIC AND LYRICS: Stephen Sondheim
BOOK: George Furth
DIRECTOR: Harold Prince
CHOREOGRAPHER: Michael Bennett
OPENED: 4/26/70, New York; a run of 705 performances

Company was the first of the Sondheim musicals to have been directed by Harold Prince, and more than any other musical reflects America in the 1970s. The show is a plotless evening about five affluent couples living in a Manhattan apartment building and their excessively protective feeling about a charming, but somewhat indifferent bachelor named Bobby.
They want to fix him up and see him married. In the end he seems ready to take the plunge. The songs are often very sophisticated, expressing the ambivalent or caustic attitudes of fashionable New Yorkers.

EVITA

MUSIC: Andrew Lloyd Webber
LYRICS: Tim Rice
DIRECTOR: Harold Prince
CHOREOGRAPHER: Larry Fuller
OPENED: 6/23/78, London; a run of 2,900 performances.   9/25/79, New York; a run of 1,567 performances

Because of its great success in London, *Evita* was practically a pre-sold hit when it began its run on Broadway. Based on the events in the life of Argentina's strong-willed leader, Eva Peron, the musical—with Patti LuPone in the title role in New York—traced her rise from struggling actress to wife of dictator Juan Peron (Bob Gunton), and virtual co-ruler of the country. Part of the concept of the show is to have a slightly misplaced Che Guevera (played by Mandy Patinkin) as a narrator and conscience to the story of Eva's quick, greedy rise to power and her early death from cancer. "I'd Be Surprisingly Good for You" is what Eva sings to Peron just a minute after their first meeting.

FUNNY GIRL

MUSIC: Jule Styne
LYRICS: Bob Merrill
BOOK: Isabel Lennart
DIRECTORS: Garson Kanin and Jerome Robbins
CHOREOGRAPHER: Carol Haney
OPENED: 3/26/64, New York; a run of 1,348 performances

The funny girl of the title refers to Fanny Brice, one of Broadway's legendary clowns, and the story, told mostly in flashback, covers her discovery by impresario Florenz Ziegfeld, her triumphs in the Ziegfeld Follies, her stormy marriage to smooth-talking con man Nick Arnstein, and the breakup of the couple after Nick has served time for stock swindling. Film producer Ray Stark, Miss Brice's son-in-law, had long wanted to make a movie based on the Fanny Brice story, but the original screenplay convinced him that it should first be done on the stage. At one time or another Mary Martin, Carol Burnett, and Anne Bancroft were announced for the leading role, but the assignment went to 22-year-old Barbra Streisand, whose only other Broadway experience had been in a supporting part in *I Can Get It for You Wholesale.* However, Streisand, through performances in clubs and on television and recording had already begun her fast ascent to stardom, and she was hardly an unknown on the opening night of *Funny Girl.* The 1968 movie version, directed by William Wyler and Herbert Ross, was Miss Streisand's auspicious film debut.

GOOD NEWS

MUSIC: Ray Henderson
LYRICS: B. G. DeSylva and Lew Brown
BOOK: Laurence Schwab and B. G. DeSylva
DIRECTOR: Edgar MacGregor
CHOREOGRAPHER: Bobby Connolly
OPENED: 9/6/27, New York; a run of 557 performances

Good News inaugurated a series of bright and breezy DeSylva, Brown and Henderson musical comedies that captured the fast-paced spirit of America's flaming youth of the 1920s. In this collegiate caper, the setting is Tait College where the student body is composed of flappers and sheiks, and where the biggest issue is whether the school's football hero will be allowed to play in the big game against Colton despite his failing grade in astronomy. It's all silly, good-natured fun. There was an unsuccessful revival on Broadway in 1974 with Alice Faye and Gene Nelson. The MGM movie version of 1947 starred June Allyson, Peter Lawford and Mel Tormé.

GREASE

MUSIC, LYRICS AND BOOK: Jim Jacobs and Warren Casey
DIRECTOR: Tom Moore
CHOREOGRAPHER: Patricia Birch
OPENED: 2/14/72, New York; a run of 3,388 performances

A surprise runaway hit reflecting the nostalgia fashion of the 1970s, *Grease* is the story of hip greaser Danny and his wholesome girl Sandy Dumbrowski; a loose plot that serves as an excuse for a light-hearted ride through the early rock 'n' roll of the 1950s. The 1978 movie version, starring John Travolta and Olivia Newton-John, is one of the top grossing musical movies of all time.

GUYS AND DOLLS

MUSIC AND LYRICS: Frank Loesser
BOOK: Abe Burrows and Jo Swerling
DIRECTOR: George S. Kaufman
CHOREOGRAPHER: Michael Kidd
OPENED: 11/24/50, New York; a run of 1,200 performances

Populated by the hard-shelled but soft-centered characters who inhabit the world of writer Damon Runyon, this "Musical Fable of Broadway" tells the tale of how Miss Sarah Brown of the Save-a-Soul Mission saves the souls of assorted Times Square riff-raff while losing her heart to the smooth-talking gambler, Sky Masterson. A more comic romance involves Nathan Detroit, who runs the "oldest established permanent floating crap game in New York," and Miss Adelaide, the star of the Hot Box nightclub (where she sings "Take Back Your Mink"), to whom he has been engaged for fourteen years, which explains her famous song, "Adelaide's Lament."

Guys and Dolls played on Broadway for 239 performances with an all black cast in 1976. In 1992, an enormously successful revival opened in New York, and a new cast recording was made of the show, with Faith Prince as Miss Adelaide. The 1955 film version stars Frank Sinatra, Marlon Brando, Jean Simmons, and Vivian Blaine (the original Miss Adelaide).

GYPSY

MUSIC: Jule Styne
LYRICS: Stephen Sondheim
BOOK: Arthur Laurents
DIRECTOR AND CHOREOGRAPHER: Jerome Robbins
OPENED: 5/21/59, New York; a run of 702 performances

Written for Ethel Merman, who gave the performance of her career as Gypsy Rose Lee's ruthless, domineering mother, *Gypsy* is one of the great scores in the mature musical comedy tradition. The idea for the musical began with producer David Merrick, who needed to read only one chapter in Miss Lee's autobiography to convince him of its stage potential. Originally, Stephen Sondheim was to have supplied the music as well as the lyrics, but Miss Merman, who had just come from a lukewarm production on Broadway, wanted the more experienced Jule Styne. In the story, Mama Rose is determined to escape from her humdrum life by pushing the vaudeville career of her daughter June. After June runs away to get married, she focuses all her attention on her other daughter, the previously neglected Louise. After a few years Louise turns into celebrated burlesque stripper Gypsy Rose Lee, and Rose suffers a breakdown when she realizes that she is no longer needed in her daughter's career ("Rose's Turn").

Gypsy also enjoyed a successful London engagement in 1973 with Angela Lansbury as Rose. This production opened in New York the following year and ran for 120 performances. Another revival, celebrating the 30th anniversary of the musical, with Tyne Daley in the Merman role, played in New York beginning in 1989 for 477 performances. (A new cast recording was released). A 1962 film version starred, alas, not Merman but Rosalind Russell.

HOUSE OF FLOWERS

MUSIC: Harold Arlen
BOOK LYRICS: Truman Capote
DIRECTOR: Peter Brook
CHOREOGRAPHER: Herbert Ross
OPENED: 12/20/54, New York; a run of 165 performances

This "musical Mardi Gras" provided a showcase for the talents of Pearl Bailey as Madame Fleur, a Carribean island madame whose "house of flowers" competed with the house of Madame Tango for the patronage of visiting sailors. Complications result when the girl Violet displays a preference for marrying her sweetheart to being sold to one of Fleur's wealthy clients. Capote wrote a short story based on his visits to the lively bordellos at Port-au-Prince, Haiti, which became the libretto for his only Broadway musical. Ottilie, originally played by Diahann Carroll, is the innocent girl who leaves the temptations of bordello life.

I CAN GET IT FOR YOU WHOLESALE

MUSIC AND LYRICS: Harold Rome
BOOK: Jerome Weidman
DIRECTOR: Arthur Laurents
CHOREOGRAPHER: Herbert Ross
OPENED: 3/22/62, New York; a run of 300 performances

Harry Bogen, the leading character in the show, is an unscrupulous conniver who uses and misuses people on his way to the top. Based on Jerome Weidman's bestselling novel, which the author adapted for the stage, the musical helped two young actors on their way to the top: Elliott Gould, who played Harry, and Barbra Streisand as the comedic, underappreciated secretary, Miss Marmelstein, in a supporting role and her Broadway debut. Set in New York's garment district in the 1930s, Harry rises in the business world through some shady deals until he finally outsmarts himself. At the end, though, there is a hint of redemption when he gets a new job and his estranged sweetheart, Ruthie, comes back to him. In "Who Knows" Ruthie is obviously trying to nudge her relationship with Harry along a bit.

MAME

MUSIC AND LYRICS: Jerry Herman
BOOK: Jerome Lawrence and Robert E. Lee
DIRECTOR: Gene Sachs
CHOREOGRAPHER: Onna White
OPENED: 5/24/66, New York; a run of 1,508 performances

Ten years after premiering the comedy based on Patrick Dennis' fictional account of his free-wheeling *Auntie Mame,* playwrights Lawrence and Lee joined forces with Jerry Herman to transform their play into a hit musical. Angela Lansbury, after years of stage and screen performances, finally achieved her stardom in the title role. The show's big ballad, "If He Walked into My Life," is sung by Mame as she thinks that she's damaged her relationship with her now-grown nephew. A 1983 revival, also starring Miss Lansbury, had a brief run on Broadway. A film version, virtually the last old-fashioned musical movie made, was released in 1974, starring Lucille Ball and Robert Preston, and from the original cast, Bea Arthur. The non-musical film of the story, *Auntie Mame,* was released in 1957 and starred Rosalind Russell.

ME AND JULIET

MUSIC: Richard Rodgers
LYRICS AND BOOK: Oscar Hammerstein II
DIRECTOR: George Abbott
CHOREOGRAPHER: Robert Alton
OPENED: 5/28/53, New York; a run of 358 performances

Me and Juliet was Rodgers and Hammerstein's valentine to show business, with its action — in *Kiss Me, Kate* fashion — taking place both backstage in a theatre and onstage during the performance of a play. Here the tale concerns a romance between a singer in the chorus and the assistant stage manager, whose newfound bliss is seriously threatened by the jealous electrician. A comic romantic subplot involves the stage manager and the principal dancer. "We Deserve Each Other" is from the play portion of the show, with contemporary Carmen and Don José characters.

MERRILY WE ROLL ALONG

MUSIC AND LYRICS: Stephen Sondheim
BOOK: George Furth
DIRECTOR: Harold Prince
CHOREOGRAPHER: Larry Fuller
OPENED: 11/16/81, New York; a run of 16 performances

Founded on the George S. Kaufman-Moss Hart play of the same name, *Merrily We Roll Along* is an innovative conception in that it tells its tale backwards—from the present when Franklin Shepard is a rich, famous, but morally compromised film producer and composer, to his idealistic youth when he graduated from high school. The story centers around the enduring and changing friendship between three people. The Broadway production was not a success, but the tuneful score has gained a following.

LES MISÉRABLES

MUSIC: Claude-Michel Schönberg
LYRICS: Herbert Kretzmer and Alain Boublil
ORIGINAL FRENCH TEXT: Alain Boublil and Jean-Marc Natel
DIRECTORS: Trevor Nunn and John Caird
CHOREOGRAPHER: Kate Flatt
OPENED: 9/80, Paris; an initial run of 3 months
          10/8/85, London; still running as of 12/9/2009
          3/12/87, New York; a run of 6,680 performances

Les Misérables lends a pop opera texture to the 1200 page Victor Hugo epic novel of social injustice and the plight of the downtrodden. The original Parisian version contained only a few songs, and many more were added when the show opened in London. Thus, most of the show's songs were originally written in English. The plot is too rich to capsulize, but centers on Jean Valjean, who has gone to prison in previous years for stealing a loaf of bread, and takes place over several years in the first half of the 19th century. "I Dreamed a Dream" is sung by Fantine, ill and dying. Cosette, secretly in love with Marius, sings "On My Own."

THE MYSTERY OF EDWIN DROOD

MUSIC, LYRICS AND BOOK: Rupert Holmes
DIRECTOR: Wilford Leach
CHOREOGRAPHER: Graciela Daniele
OPENED: 12/2/85, New York; a run of 608 performances

Rupert Holmes' lifelong fascination with Charles Dickens' unfinished novel was the catalyst for the play. Since there were no clues as to Drood's murderer or even if a murder had been committed, Holmes decided to let the audience provide the show's ending by voting how it turns out. The writer's second major decision was to offer the musical as if it were being performed by an acting company at London's Music Hall Royale in 1873, complete with such conventions as a Chairman (George Rose) to comment on the action and a woman (Betty Buckley) to play the part of Edwin Drood. The show was notable for the appearance of jazz legend Cleo Laine as the eccentric and mysterious Princess Puffer. On November 13, 1986, in an attempt to attract more theatre-goers, the musical's title was changed to *Drood*.

NINE

MUSIC AND LYRICS: Maury Yeston
BOOK: Arthur Kopit, Mario Fratti
DIRECTOR: Tommy Tune
CHOREOGRAPHERS: Tommy Tune and Thommie Walsh
OPENED: 5/9/82, New York; a run of 732 performances

The influence of the director-choreographer was emphasized again with Tommy Tune's highly stylized, visually striking production of *Nine*, which, besides being a feast for the eyes is also one of the very few non-Sondheim Broadway scores to have true musical substance and merit from the 1970s and 1980s. The musical evolved from Yeston's fascination with Federico Fellini's semi-autobiographical 1963 film *8 1/2*. The story spotlights Guido Contini, a celebrated but tormented director in a mid-life crisis who has come to a Venetian spa for a rest, and his relationships with his wife, his mistress, his protégé, his producer, and his mother. Luisa, Guido's wife, sings about her unusual husband near the beginning of the show in "My Husband Makes Movies."

NO STRINGS

MUSIC AND LYRICS: Richard Rodgers
BOOK: Samuel Taylor
DIRECTOR & CHOREOGRAPHER: Joe Layton
OPENED: 3/15/62, New York; a run of 580 performances

Richard Rodgers' first musical after the death of his partner, Oscar Hammerstein II, and the only Broadway production in his long career for which the composer also served as his own lyricist. *No Strings* offered such innovations as hiding the orchestra backstage, featuring instrumentalists onstage to accompany the singers, having the principals and chorus move scenery and props in full view of the audience, and—to conform to the play's title—eliminating the orchestra's string section. The libretto is of a love affair between a fashion model (Diahann Carroll), and a former Pulitzer Prize-winning novelist, now a "Europe bum" (Richard Kiley). In the end, after enjoying the good life in Monte Carlo, Honfleur, Deauville, and St. Tropez, the writer, with no strings attached, returns home to the U.S. Though because of casting, the show was about an interracial romance, this was never commented on in the script. "The Sweetest Sounds" opens the show, sung as a kind of an overture to the evening.

OLIVER!

MUSIC, LYRICS AND BOOK: Lionel Bart
DIRECTOR: Peter Coe
OPENED: 6/30/60, London; a run of 2,618 performances; 1/6/63, New York; a run of 744 performances

Oliver! established Lionel Bart as Britain's outstanding musical theatre talent of the 1960s when the musical opened in London. Until overtaken by *Jesus Christ Superstar*, *Oliver!* set the record as the longest-running musical in British history. Based on Charles Dickens' novel about the orphan Oliver Twist and his adventures as one of Fagin's pickpocketing crew, *Oliver!* also had the longest run of any British musical presented in New York in the 1960s. The show was revived on Broadway in 1984. In 1968, it was made into an Academy Award-winning movie produced by Columbia. "As Long As He Needs Me" is Nancy's song about her rough and abusive man, Bill Sykes.

ON THE TOWN

MUSIC: Leonard Bernstein
BOOK AND LYRICS: Betty Comden and Adolph Green
DIRECTOR: George Abbott
CHOREOGRAPHER: Jerome Robbins
OPENED: 12/28/44, New York; a run of 463 performances

This major show was the Broadway debut of some very major talents: composer Leonard Bernstein, choreographer Jerome Robbins, and writers Betty Comden and Adolph Green. It was based on the Robbins-Bernstein ballet from the previous year, *Fancy Free*. The story is of three sailors on a 24 hour leave in New York City. They each meet a girl, of course. One of the boys, Chip, meets a cab driver named Hildy. They hit it off. Hildy brings Chip to her apartment, and is anxious to show off her relationship qualifications, and by the way, she can cook too. The 1949 film version largely replaced Bernstein's score.

ONCE UPON A MATTRESS

MUSIC: Mary Rodgers
LYRICS: Marshall Barer
BOOK: Jay Thompson, Dean Fuller and Marshall Barer
DIRECTOR: George Abbott
CHOREOGAPHER: Joe Layton
OPENED: 5/11/59, New York; a run of 460 performances

Once Upon a Mattress was first created as a one act musical by Mary Rodgers (daughter of Richard Rodgers) and Marshall Barer at an adult summer camp. They expanded the work, based on the fairy tale "The Princess and the Pea," into a full evening's entertainment that is notable as the stage debut of Carol Burnett as Princess Winnifred. Queen Agravain has ruled that her son will only marry someone of royal blood. Winnifred spends a sleepless night, disturbed by one lone pea, planted by the queen, under a pile of mattresses. Actually, an accomplice had secretly stuffed the bed with an arsenol of uncomfortability. In "Shy" Princess Winnifred introduces herself.

PETER PAN

MUSIC: Mark Charlap, additional music by Jule Styne
LYRICS: Carolyn Leigh, additional lyrics by Betty Comden and Adolph Green
DIRECTOR AND CHOREOGRAPHER: Jerome Robbins
OPENED: 10/20/54, New York; a run of 152 performances

Although many actresses have portrayed Peter Pan in almost as many productions, Mary Martin and this version of the story are perhaps the best known and loved. In spite of a modest run on Broadway, this production found a vast new audience through numerous television broadcasts. Peter Pan was first presented in New York in 1905 with Maude Adams as Peter, revived in 1924 with Marilyn Miller, who added two Jerome Kern songs to the show. In 1950 Jean Arthur played Peter to Boris Karloff's Captain Hook, with five songs by Leonard Bernstein. A 1979 revival of the 1954 musical ran 551 performances and starred Sandy Duncan.

PLAIN AND FANCY

MUSIC: Albert Hague
LYRICS: Arnold B. Horwitt
BOOK: Joseph Stein and Will Glickman
DIRECTOR: Morton Da Costa
CHOREOGRAPHER: Helen Tamiris
OPENED: 1/27/55, New York; a run of 461 performances

The setting of *Plain and Fancy* was Amish country in Pennsylvania, where two worldly New Yorkers (Richard Derr and Shirl Conway) have gone to sell a farm they had inherited—but not before they had a chance to meet the God-fearing people and appreciate their simple but unyielding way of living. The warm and atmospheric score was composed by Albert Hague, familiar to television viewers as the bearded music teacher in the series *Fame*.

THE SECRET GARDEN

MUSIC: Lucy Simon
LYRICS AND BOOK: Marsha Norman
DIRECTOR: Susan H. Schulman
CHOREOGRAPHER: Michael Lichtefeld
OPENED: 4/25/91, New York; 706 performances

Based on the novel by Frances Hodgson Burnett, the story is of an orphaned child, Mary Lennox, who is sent to live with her uncle Archibald in Yorkshire in the nineteenth century. He is absorbed in grief over the death of his young wife ten years earlier, and the house is gloomy and mysterious. Mary finds her dead aunt's "secret garden," passionately nurtures it to life, and Archie also comes back to life once he can let go of his grief. The song "Hold On" is sung by the warm and caring servant Martha, in her local Yorkshire accent, to the frightened and insecure Mary.

SHE LOVES ME

MUSIC: Jerry Bock
LYRICS: Sheldon Harnick
BOOK: Joe Masteroff
DIRECTOR: Harold Prince
CHOREOGRAPHER: Carol Haney
OPENED: 4/23/63, New York; a run of 301 performances

The closely integrated, melody drenched score of *She Loves Me* is certainly one of the best ever written for a musical comedy. It was based on a Hungarian play, *Parfumerie*, by Miklos Laszlo, that had already been used as the basis for two films, *The Shop Around the Corner* and *In the Good Old Summertime* (with a change of locale to the U.S.) Set in the 1930s in what could only be Budapest, the tale is of the people who work in Maraczek's Parfumerie, principally the constantly quabbling sales clerk Amalia Balash (Barbara Cook) and the manager Georg Nowack (Daniel Massey). It is soon revealed that they are anonymous pen pals who agree to meet one night at the Café Imperiale, though neither knows the other's identity. Ilona is an illiterate clerk at the store, a comic but attractive recipient of the attention of men. Taking the advice of her friend, Amalia, she makes a trip to the library, and well...The musical is well represented on the original cast album, which on two disks preserves practically every note of the show's music.

SONG AND DANCE

MUSIC: Andrew Lloyd Webber
LYRICS: Don Black, Richard Maltby Jr.
ADAPTATION: Richard Maltby Jr.
DIRECTOR: Richard Maltby Jr.
CHOREOGRAPHER: Peter Martins
OPENED: 9/18/85, New York; a run of 474 performances

The "Dance" of the title originated in 1979 when Andrew Lloyd Webber composed a set of variations on Paganini's A minor Capriccio that seemed to him to be perfect for a ballet. The "Song" originated a year later with a one-woman television show, *Tell Me on a Sunday*, which consisted entirely of musical pieces. Two years after that both works were presented together in London as a full evening's entertainment, now connected with a bit of plot. In New York, this unconventional package won high praise for Bernadette Peters, whose task in Act I was to create, without dialogue or other actors, the character of a free-spirited English girl who has dalliances in America with four men.

SUNDAY IN THE PARK WITH GEORGE

MUSIC AND LYRICS: Stephen Sondheim
BOOK AND DIRECTION: James Lapine
OPENED: 5/2/84, New York; a run of 604 performances

The centerpiece of this ambitious show is George Seurat's great painting "A Sunday Afternoon on the Island of La Grande Jatte." It is an intimate and personal musical concerned with the creative process itself, its obsessions, consequences, and rewards. The piece received the Pulitzer Prize for drama in 1985. An adaptation of the Broadway production (starring Mandy Patinkin and Bernadette Peters) was made for television, and is available for purchase on videotape. "Everybody Loves Louis," sung by Dot after she and George have split up, is about her new beau, Louis, the baker.

THEY'RE PLAYING OUR SONG

MUSIC: Marvin Hamlisch
LYRICS: Carole Bayer Sager
BOOK: Neil Simon
DIRECTOR: Robert Moore
CHOREOGRAPHER: Patricia Birch
OPENED: 2/11/79, New York; a run of 1,082 performances

They're Playing Our Song was based in part on composer Marvin Hamlisch's often tempestuous romance with lyricist Carole Bayer Sager. In the quasi-drame à clef musical, Vernon Gersch, a wise-cracking neurotic song writer, and Sonia Walsk, a wise-cracking, neurotic lyric writer, try to have both a professional and personal relationship, despite constant interruptions caused by telephone calls from Sonia's former lover. To tell their story, the authors hit upon the notion of having only two real characters in the musical, though each has three singing alter egos, and their songs express how they feel about their work as well as about each other.

VICTOR/VICTORIA

MUSIC: Henry Mancini; additonal musical material by Frank Wildhorn
LYRICS: Leslie Bricusse
BOOK: Blake Edwards
DIRECTOR: Blake Edwards
CHOREOGRAPHER: Rob Marshall
OPENED: 10/25/95, New York; a run of 734 performances

After a 35-year absence, Julie Andrews made her ballyhooed return to Broadway in this stage adaptation of her 1982 film musical, directed and co-written by her husband, Blake Edwards. Desperate for a job in Depression-era Paris, singer Victoria (Andrews) is persuaded by her friend, the aging self-described "drag queen" Toddy, to pose as a female impersonator named Victor—making her a woman pretending to be a man pretending to be a woman. (S)he's a smash, and attracts the attentions of a Chicago gangster who feels strangely attracted to "Victor." The gangster's randy girlfriend tries to rekindle his interest with the comically bawdy "Paris Makes Me Horny," running down a list of other cities and what they're good for—but always returning to the title refrain.

THERE WON'T BE TRUMPETS

from *Anyone Can Whistle*

Words and Music by
STEPHEN SONDHEIM

see! _____ There won't be

trum - pets or bolts of fi - re To say he's com - ing.

No Ro - man can - dles, No an - gels'

choir,_ No sound of dis - tant drum - ming.

He may ___ not be the cav - a - lier, Tall and ___

___ grace - ful, Fair and ___ strong. Does - n't mat - ter ___

___ just as long as he comes a - long! _____ But

Marcia *(accel. poco ma non troppo)*

not with trum - pets or light - ning flash - es Or

20

min - ute you turn and he's sud - den - ly there,

Faster (♩ = 88)

You won't need trum - pets!

There are no trum - pets!

Who needs trum - pets?

I GET A KICK OUT OF YOU

from *Anything Goes*

Words and Music by
COLE PORTER

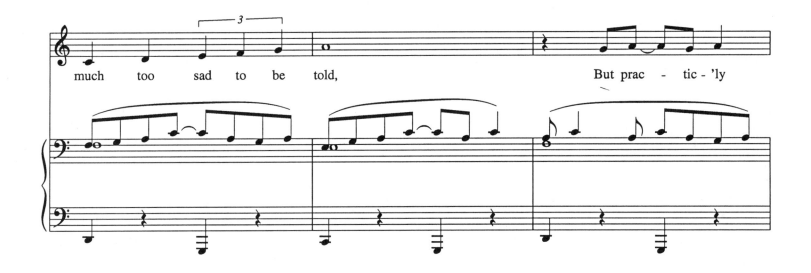

THE GENTLEMAN IS A DOPE

from *Allegro*

Lyrics by OSCAR HAMMERSTEIN II
Music by RICHARD RODGERS

else - 's prob - lem, _____ She's wel - come

to the guy! _____ She'll nev - er

un - der - stand _ him _____ half as well

as I. _____ The gen-tle-man is a dope_

33

I WISH I WERE IN LOVE AGAIN
from *Babes in Arms*

Lyrics by LORENZ HART
Music by RICHARD RODGERS

This is a duet in the show.

love-ly lov-ing and the hate-ful hates, The con-ver-sa-tion with the fly-ing plates, I

wish I were in love a-gain! No_ more pain, No_ more

strain, Now_ I'm sane but_ I would rath-er be ga-ga!_ The

pulled out fur of cat and cur, The fine mis-mat-ing of a him and her, I've

With freedom

learned my les - son, but I wish I were in love a - gain.

ad lib.

You don't know that I felt good _ when we up and part - ed. _ You don't know I

knocked on wood, _ glad - ly bro - ken heart - ed. _ Wor - ry - ing is through, I sleep all night _

Ap - pe - tite and health re - stored. You don't know how much I'm bored!

a tempo

(Tempo primo)

The fur-tive sigh, The black-ened eye, The words "I'll love you till the

day I die," The self de-cep-tion that be-lieves the lie, I wish I were in

love a-gain! When love con-geals it soon re-veals the faint a-ro-ma of per-

form-ing seals, The dou-ble cross-ing of a pair of heels, I wish I were in

JOHNNY ONE NOTE

from *Babes in Arms*

Words by LORENZ HART
Music by RICHARD RODGERS

mute, _____ John - ny stood a - lone.

Cats and dogs stopped yap - ping, Li - ons in the

zoo all _ were jeal - ous _ at John - ny's _ big

trill. _____ Thun - der claps

Sing, John - ny one note, — Sing out — with gus - to, — And just o - ver - whelm all — the crowd. —

(W. W.)

(simile)

(W. W.)

(Br.)

Ah! —
(W. W. unis.)

f (Br. simile)

FIFTY PERCENT
from *Ballroom*

Lyrics by ALAN and MARILYN BERGMAN
Music by BILLY GOLDENBERG

THE PARTY'S OVER

from *Bells Are Ringing*

Words by BETTY COMDEN and ADOLPH GREEN
Music by JULE STYNE

He's in love with Mel - i - sande Scott, A

girl who does-n't ex - ist. He's in love with some-one you're not, and

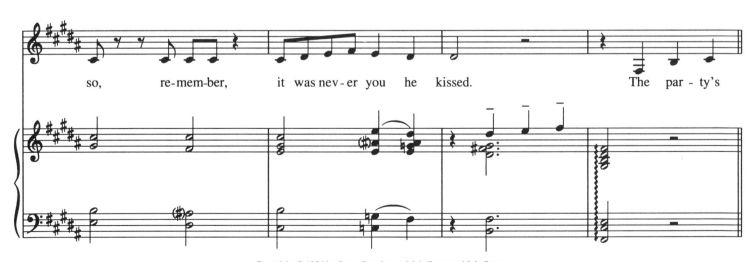

so, re-mem-ber, it was nev-er you he kissed. The par-ty's

o - ver. It's time to call it a day. _____ No mat - ter

how you pre-tend, you knew it would end this way. It's time to wind up

the mas-quer - ade. Just make your mind up the pi - per

must be paid. The par - ty's o - ver, The can - dles flick - er and dim. _____

poco rit.   *a tempo*   *p*

You danced and dreamed through the night; It seemed to be right, just be-ing with him.

Now you must wake up; All dreams must end.

Take off your make-up. The par-ty's o-ver; It's all

o-ver, my friend.

LONG BEFORE I KNEW YOU
from *Bells Are Ringing*

Lyrics by BETTY COMDEN
and ADOLPH GREEN
Music by JULE STYNE

Moderately

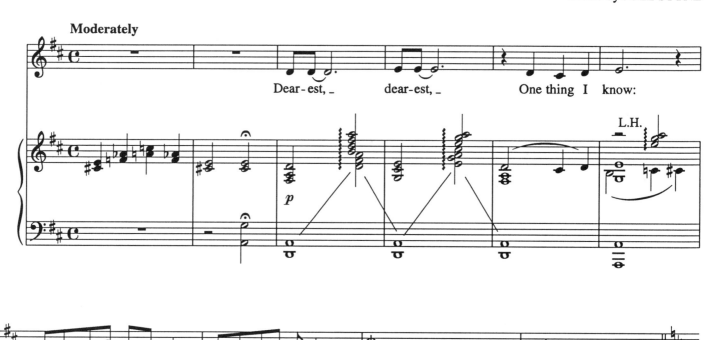

Dear-est, _ dear-est, _ One thing I know:

Ev-'ry-thing I feel for you start-ed man-y a-ges a - go. _

Long be-fore I knew you, _ Long be-fore I met you, _

*In the show Ella sings portions of this song, but never the entire number.

Long be-fore I touched you___ and felt this glow.___

But now you real - ly are here and

now at last I know That long be-fore I knew you, ___

___ I loved you so.

SOMEONE ELSE'S STORY
from *Chess*

Words and Music by
BENNY ANDERSSON, TIM RICE
and BJORN ULVAEUS

Slow 8 - Beat Ballad

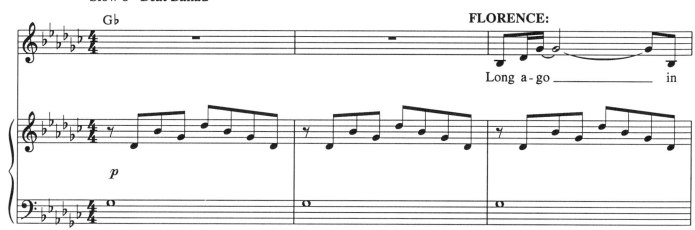

Long a-go _____ in

some-one el-se's life - time, some-one with my name ___ who looked _ a lot _ like me _

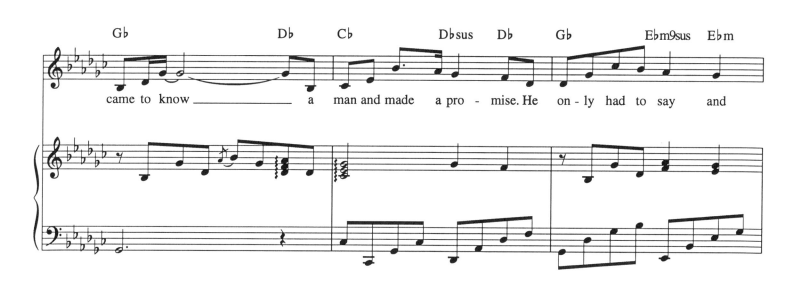

came to know _____ a man and made a pro - mise. He on-ly had to say and

WHAT I DID FOR LOVE
from *A Chorus Line*

Lyrics by EDWARD KLEBAN
Music by MARVIN HAMLISCH

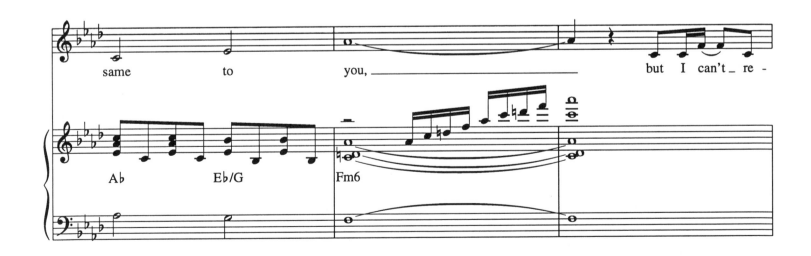

69

ANOTHER HUNDRED PEOPLE

from *Company*

Music and Lyrics by
STEPHEN SONDHEIM

Allegretto (♩ = 112)
(dolce e leggiero)

An-oth-er hun-dred peo-ple just got off of the train _ and came up through the ground _ while an-

oth-er hun-dred peo-ple just got off of the bus _ and are look-ing a-round _ at an-

oth-er hun-dred peo-ple who got off of the plane _ and are look-ing at us _ who got

off of the train __ and the plane and the bus __ may - be yes-ter-day. ___

It's a ci - ty of strang - ers. ___

Some come to work, some __ to play. __ A ci - ty of strang - ers, ___

Some come to stare, some __ to stay. ___ And

ev - 'ry day _____ the ones who stay _____

can find each oth - er in the crowd - ed streets and the

guard - ed parks, _____ By the rust - y foun - tains and the

dust - y trees with the bat - tered barks, _____ And they

(poco cresc.)

mp

gliss.

74

THE MUSIC THAT MAKES ME DANCE

from *Funny Girl*

Words by BOB MERRILL
Music by JULE STYNE

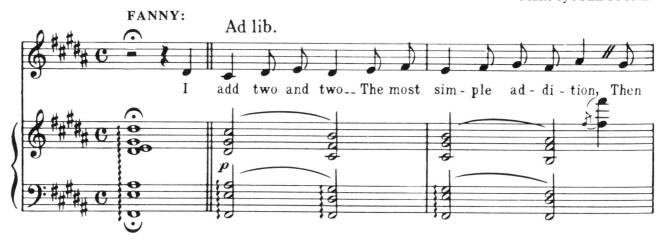

I add two and two__ The most sim-ple ad-di-tion, Then

swear that the fig-ures are ly-ing. I'm a much bet-ter com-ic than

math-e-ma-ti-cian 'Cause I'm bet-ter on stage than at in-ter-mis-sion. And as

far as the man is con - cerned... If I've been burned, I have-n't

learned.

Slowly - In tempo

I

Moderately slow 4

know he's a - round when the sky and the ground start in ring - ing. ___

I know when he's near by the thun - der I hear in ad-

vance. His words and his words a-lone are the

words that can start my heart sing-ing. ——— And

his is the on-ly mu-sic that makes me dance. ———

——— He'll sleep and he'll rise in the light of two eyes that a-

dore him.　　　　　　　Bore him it might, But he

won't leave my sight for a glance.　　　In ev-'ry

way, ev-'ry day, I need less of my-self And need more him__

Ad lib.

more him._____ 'Cause his is the on - ly mu - sic that makes me

colla voce

dance._____ 'Cause his is the on - ly

Br.

fz

p

mu - sic that makes me dance!_____

ff

I'D BE SURPRISINGLY GOOD FOR YOU

from *Evita*

Lyrics by TIM RICE
Music by ANDREW LLOYD WEBBER

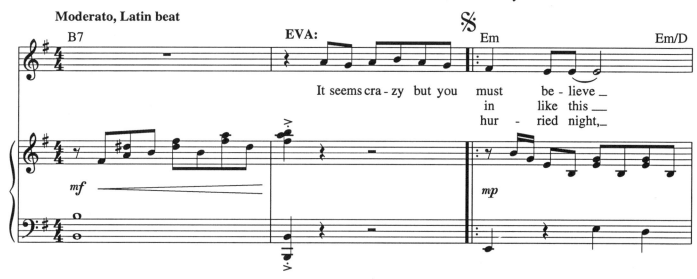

The accompaniment has been written out as a simple suggestion of the style.
It's most appropriate for the pianist to improvise in a gentle Latin style.

MCA music publishing

I WANT TO BE BAD
from *Good News*

Lyrics and Music by
B.G. DeSYLVA, LEW BROWN
and RAY HENDERSON

Good or bad which is the best for me?

When you're af-ter fun and laugh-ter This ag-gra-vates you

Some re-form-er says a warm-er cli-mate a-waits you.

Refrain

If it's naugh-ty to rouge your lips Shake your shoul-ders and twist your hips

Let a la-dy con-fess I want to be bad

If it's naught-y to vamp the men Sleep each morn-ing till af-ter ten

Then the an-swer is "yes, I want to be bad." This thing of

be-ing a good lit-tle "Good-ie" is all ver-y well.

marcato
cresc.

What can you do if your load-ed with plent-y Of hell - th ____ and vig - or? When you're learn-ing what lips are for ___ If it's naught-y to ask for more ___ Let a la - dy con - fess I want ___ to be bad.

1. bad.

2. bad. ____

LOOK AT ME, I'M SANDRA DEE

from *Grease*

Lyric and Music by WARREN CASEY
and JIM JACOBS

(20th-Century Fox theme)

Moderate 3 (♩. = 58)

* Sung an octave lower than written

filth - y paws off my silk - y drawers, would you pull that

stuff with An - nette?   As   for   you,   Troy

Don - a - hue,   I   know   what   you   wan - na

ADELAIDE'S LAMENT
from *Guys and Dolls*

By FRANK LOESSER

person ___ can de-vel-op a cold   You can spray her wher-ev-er you fig-ure the strept-o-
person ___ can de-vel-op a cough.   You can feed her all day with the Vi-ta-min A and the

-coc-ci   lurk, ___   You can give her a shot for what-ev-er she's got but it just won't work ___   If she's
Bro-mo   Fizz ___   But the med-i-cine nev-er gets an-y-where near where the trou-ble is. ___   If she's

tir-ed of get-ting the fish-eye   from the   ho-tel   clerk, ___   A
get-ting a kind of   a name for her-self and the   name   ain't "his" ___   A

person ___ can de-vel-op a cold. (It says here) The   And
person ___ can de-vel-op a   cough.

1 (resumes reading)   *2*

fur-ther-more_ just from stall-ing and stall-ing And stall-ing the wed-ding trip, A

ten. *with sweet meditation*

per-son_ can de-vel-op La grippe. When they get on the train for Ni-ag-'ra and she can hear

suddenly angry

church bells chime_ The com-part-ment is air con-di-tioned_and the mood sub-lime_ Then they

pp

get off at Sa-ra-to-ga for the four-teenth time,_ A per-son_ can de-vel-op La

grippe, (Hm!) La grippe, La post na-sal drip With the whee-zes and the sneezes and a

poco rit. *a tempo*

si-nus that's real-ly a pip! From a lack of com-mu-ni-ty pro-per-ty___ and a

feel-ing she's get-ting too old, A per-son can de-vel-op a

bad bad cold.___

SMALL WORLD

from *Gypsy*

Words by STEPHEN SONDHEIM
Music by JULE STYNE

98

PARIS MAKES ME HORNY
from *Victor/Victoria*

Words by LESLIE BRICUSSE
Music by HENRY MANCINI

Lyrics (under the staves):

Par - is makes me horn - y.

Rome may be hot, sex - y it is not. Par - is is so sex - y.
As for Ma-drid, save it for El Cid. Din - in' at the Li - do

I NEVER HAS SEEN SNOW

from *House of Flowers*

Lyrics by TRUMAN CAPOTE
and HAROLD ARLEN
Music by HAROLD ARLEN

A stone rolled off my heart when I laid my eyes on

that near to me boy with that far a-way look,__ and right from the start,__ I

saw a new hor-i-zon and a road to take me where I want-ed to be took,__

need-ed to be took,__ and

espr.

a tempo

8va

WHO KNOWS
from *I Can Get It For You Wholesale*

Words and Music by
HAROLD ROME

Freely

RUTHIE:

New York is a won-der-ful town, A ver-y stim-u-lat-ing place to be. It's full of gal-ler-ies and ex-hi-bi-tions, Most are ab-so-lute-ly free, And con-certs like at Lew-is-ohn sta-di-um, plus at Car-ne-gie hall. We sit 'way up top, but it's won-der-ful a-cous-tics. That's where it sounds best of

all. Art lec-tures at the Met-ro-pol-i-tan. I at-

tend-ed an-cient Greece the oth-er day. The mod-ern dance and

Fls.

bal-let at the Y. M. and Dou-ble-u H. A. And le-git-i-mate plays on

Broad-way. Don't you think O-dets is great? Not down stairs, of course, We get

112

why   it will be him, who knows?

Str.

Perfect he does-n't have to be, good look-ing or rich and smart.

Str., W.W.

Long as he's cra - zy af-ter me, And we see heart to heart. Who

rall.

knows   when he'll be there, who knows?   One

W.W.

L.H.   L.H.

Str.

a tempo

day he'll see me there and hold out his arms.

Tempo rubato

First he'll kiss me, Say he loves me. And then pro - pose! But

why, where, when, Who knows?

IF HE WALKED INTO MY LIFE
from *Mame*

Music and Lyric by
JERRY HERMAN

Where's that boy with the bu - gle?

My lit-tle love Who was al - ways my big ro - mance.

Tpt. Solo

W. W.

Hp. gliss.

Where's that boy with the bu - gle? And why did I ev - er

Bells, Hp.

Str. (cued for W.W.)

bossed him? _____ What a shame I nev - er real - ly found the

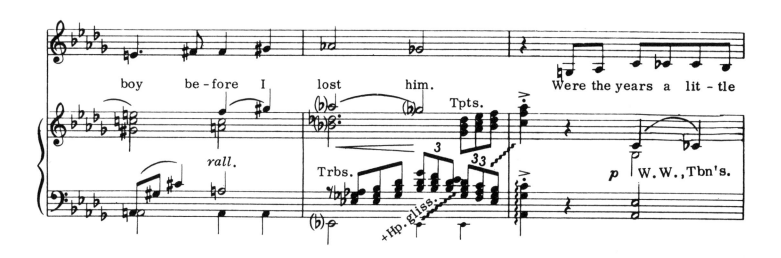

boy be - fore I lost him. Were the years a lit - tle

fast? _____ Was his world a lit - tle free? _____

Was there too much of a crowd, All too lush and loud And not e-nough of

W.W.,Str.

me? Tpts Tho' I'll ask my-self my whole life long,

Str. (cued for W.W.) Cello, Hp.

(cued for Bs.Cl.)

What went wrong a-long the way? Would I make the same mis-

Bells Cel.

+Cl.

122

WE DESERVE EACH OTHER

from *Me and Juliet*

Lyrics by OSCAR HAMMERSTEIN II
Music by RICHARD RODGERS

Moderato

We de-serve each oth-er, We de-serve each oth-er,

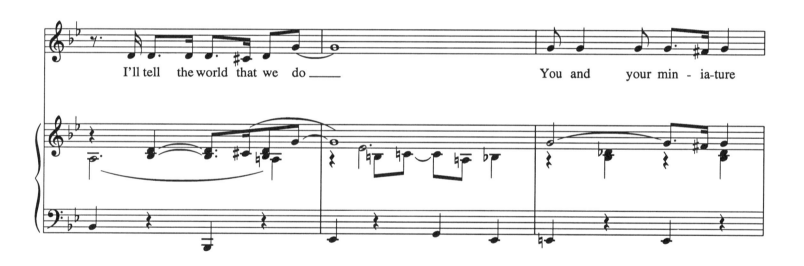

I'll tell the world that we do ____ You and your min - ia-ture

spar - row brain, _ I and my ti - ny I. Q. We de-serve each oth-er,

Let me tell you, broth-er, I am a dif - fi-cult girl. ___

You're an im-pos - si-ble char - ac - ter, ___ Why don't we give it a

whirl? I don't want __ to re - form you, ___ To

make your mis - takes __ you are free. But I just want __ to be

cer - tain ___ that your great-est mis-take will be me!

If you want to wres-tle, I'm the weak-er ves-sel, And I'll be eas - y to swerve, ___

___ We de - serve each oth - er, ___ So

let us take what we de - serve.

NOW YOU KNOW

from *Merrily We Roll Along*

Music and Lyrics by
STEPHEN SONDHEIM

MARY:

All right, now you know: _

Life is crum - my. Well, now you know. _ I mean,

big sur - prise: Peo - ple love _ you and tell you lies.

saints get shot,__ It's called God don't an - swer prayers a lot, __ O - kay,

now you know._____

O - kay, now you know, __ Now for - get it. Don't

fall a - part __ at the seams. It's called let - ting go __ your il -

129

I DREAMED A DREAM
from *Les Misérables*

Lyrics by HERBERT KRETZMER
Original Text by ALAIN BOUBLIL and JEAN-MARC NATEL
Music by CLAUDE-MICHEL SCHÖNBERG

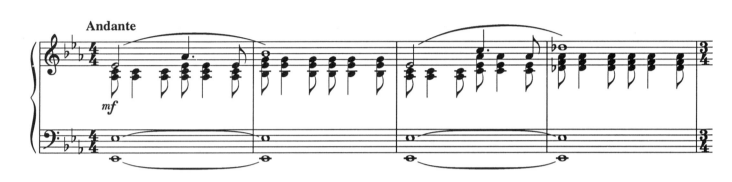

And the song was ex -cit -ing.   There was a time.   Then it all went wrong.

Andante

FANTINE:

I dreamed a dream in time gone by   When hope   was high and life worth

liv - ing,   I dreamed   that love would nev - er   die,

134

I dreamed that God would be for - giv - ing. Then I was young and un - af -

raid And dreams were made and used and wast-ed.

There was no ran - som to be paid, No song un-sung, no wine un -

Poco più mosso

tast - ed. But the ti - gers come at night

mf

136

ON MY OWN
from *Les Misérables*

Lyrics by HERBERT KRETZMER, JOHN CAIRD and TREVOR NUNN
Original Text by ALAIN BOUBLIL and JEAN-MARC NATEL
Music by CLAUDE-MICHEL SCHÖNBERG

EPONINE:

And now I'm all a-lone a-gain, no-where to go, no one to turn to.

I did not want your mon-ey sir, I came out here 'cos I was told to, And now the night is

near, Now I can make be - lieve he's here.

Some-times I walk a-lone at night when ev-ery-bod-y else is sleep - ing,

I think of him and then I'm hap-py with the com-pa-ny I'm keep - ing. The ci - ty goes to

rall.　　　　　　　　　　　　**Andante**

bed　　And I can live in - side my head.

On my own,　　pre - tend - ing he's be -
rain,　　the pave - ment shines like

side _ me,　　All a - lone I walk with him 'til
sil - ver,　　All the lights are mis - ty in the

morn - ing.　　With - out him I feel his arms a -
riv - er.　　In the dark - ness, the trees are full of

141

142

THE WAGES OF SIN
from *The Mystery of Edwin Drood*

Words and Music by
RUPERT HOLMES

145

Rubato

off it! Who would buy this sack of skin? On the whole there ain't much

pro - fit in the wa - ges of sin, in the wa - ges of

mf *mp* *a tempo* *rit.*

sin, in _____ the wa - ges of sin! I've seen

rit.

Tempo I

girls from gut - ter fam' - lies trap rich men wiv flut - t'ry ways, and they

mp

MY HUSBAND MAKES MOVIES

from *Nine*

Lyrics and Music by
MAURY YESTON

Tempo II (♩ = 68)
mp

Gui - do Con - ti - ni, Lu - i - sa Con - ti - ni; num - ber one gen - ius and num - ber one fan.

Gui - do Con - ti - ni, Lu - i - sa Con - ti - ni; daugh-ter of well - to-do Flor - en - tine clan long a -

go twen-ty years a - go. Once the names were

rit.

a tempo

Gui - do Con - ti - ni, Lu - i - sa Del For - no; ac - tress with dreams and a life of her own,

a tempo

Pas-sion-ate, wild, and in love in Li-vor-no, sing-ing with Gui-do all night on the phone long a-

go some-one else a - go. How he needs me

so, and he'll be the last to know it. My

Tempo I

hus - band makes mov - ies. To

some re - tire ___ ear - ly when they've seen the eve - ning news. My

hus - band on - ly rare - ly comes to bed my

rit.

hus - band makes mov - ies, in - stead. My

Tempo II

hus - band makes mov - ies. . .

8va bassa

THE SWEETEST SOUNDS
from *No Strings*

Lyrics and Music by
RICHARD RODGERS

The verse does not appear in the show, but was written by Mr. Rodgers for the song to stand alone.

dear - est love in all the world Is wait - ing some-where for

me, _____ Is wait - ing some - where, some - where for

me.

The sweet - est sounds I'll

159

160

I CAN COOK TOO

from *On the Town*

Words and Music by LEONARD BERNSTEIN
Additional Choruses by BETTY COMDEN and ADOLPH GREEN

Oh, I can cook, too,_ on top of the rest,_ My

sea-food's the best_ in the town. Yes, I can cook, too,_ My

162

165

168

[Interlude]

Ba - by, I'm cook-in' with gas.___ Oh, I'm a

AS LONG AS HE NEEDS ME
from the Columbia Pictures-Romulus film *Oliver!*

Words and Music by
LIONEL BART

171

Tempo I

172

play This game his way_____ As long as

he needs me___ I know where I must be___ I'll cling on stead-fast-

-ly___ As long as he needs me___ As long as life is long__ I'll love him

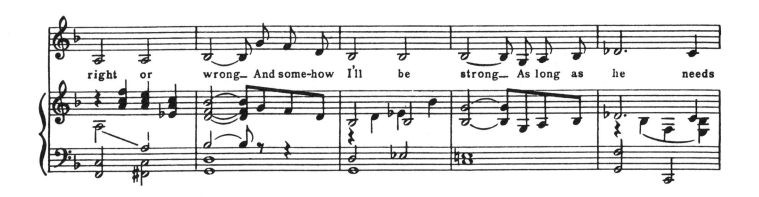

right or wrong___ And some-how I'll be strong___ As long as he needs

SHY
from *Once Upon a Mattress*

Words by MARSHALL BARER
Music by MARY RODGERS

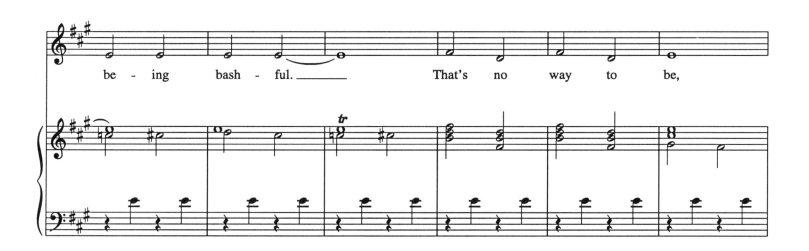

strong _____ but as weak as I am, All I can do is try. God knows I

try! _____ Though I'm fright-ened and shy _____

_____ And de - spite the im - pres - sion I give, I con - fess that I'm liv - ing a

lie, _____ Be - cause I'm ac - tual - ly ter - ri - bly ti - mid and hor - ri - bly

Rubato

Moderate 2

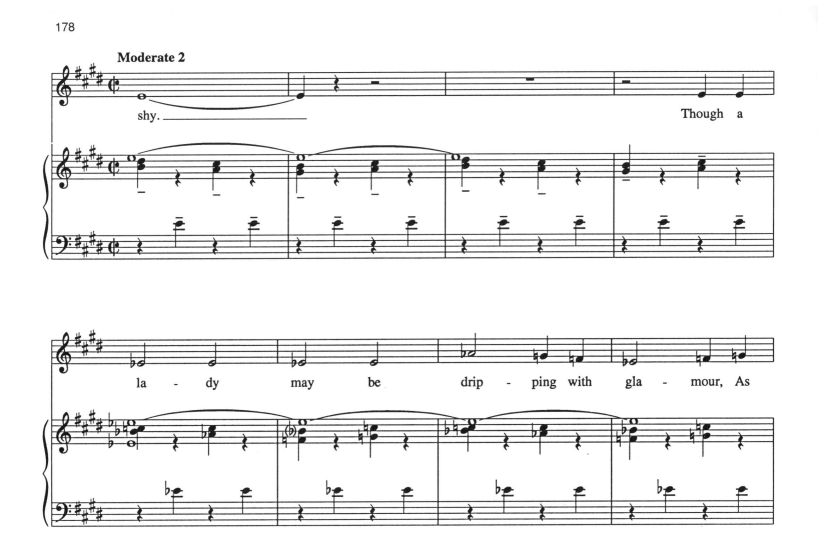

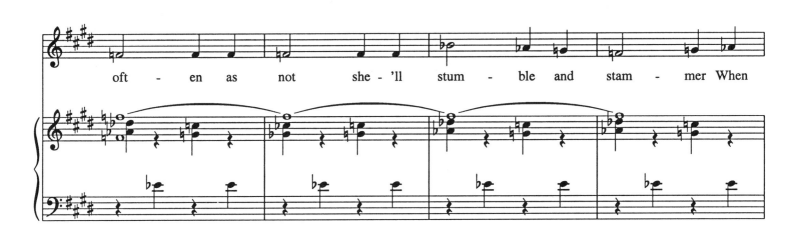

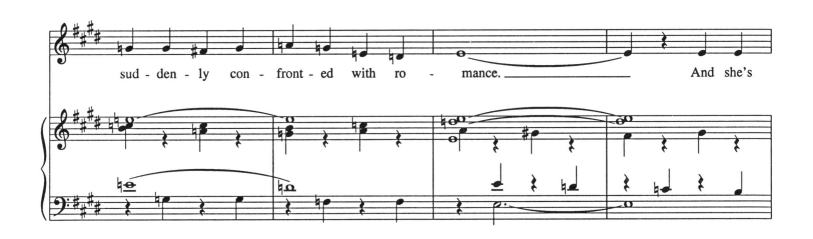

like - ly to fall on her face _____ When she's

fi - nal - ly face to face with a pair of pants.

Quite oft - en the la - dy's not as

hard to please as she seems. _____ Quite

oft - en she'll set - tle for some - thing less than the man of her

dreams. ____

I'm go - ing fish - ing for a mate.

mp

mf

I'm gon - na look in ev - 'ry nook.

mf

Where, sir ___ And when, sir? ___ I could-n't ___ be ten - ser, ___ So

Let's get ___ this done, man. ___ Get on with ___ the fun, man.

I am one man shy. ___

Jazz 4

IT'S A HELLUVA WAY TO
RUN A LOVE AFFAIR

from *Plain and Fancy*

Words by ARNOLD B. HORWITT
Music by ALBERT HAGUE

184

Bounce tempo

-o!

He may a - dore me how would I know?

If I'm the light of his life _____ It does-n't show. _____ I go through the

mo-tions but I'm well a - ware It's a hell-u-va way to run a love af-

-fair. _____

He does-n't tin-gle when-ev-er we meet _____

Our love has all of the thrill _____ Of shredded wheat _____ We

nev - er run bare-foot through each oth - er's hair It's a hell-u-va way to

run a love af - fair! _____
1. Some luck-y lov-ers have a
2. One en-chant-ed eve-ning in my

ta - lent for ro - mance,   Hack-en-sack can seem like Par-is France. _____
qui - et liv - ing room,   Can-dle lit and hea-vy with per - fume. _____

-ware? It's a hell-u-va way to run a love af-fair.

D.%

2 (Coda)

C'est la guerre! My trust-worth-y, loy-al, help-ful, friend-ly,

square, It's a hell-u-va way to run a love af-

-fair!

NEVER NEVER LAND
from *Peter Pan*

Lyrics by BETTY COMDEN
and ADOLPH GREEN
Music by JULE STYNE

189

190

HOLD ON
from *The Secret Garden*

Lyrics by MARSHA NORMAN
Music by LUCY SIMON

MARTHA:

What you've got to do is fin - ish what you have be - gun.

I don't know just how, but it's not o - ver 'til you've won. When you

ask how long or why, child, hold on to what you know is true, hold on 'til you get through.

Child, oh child, hold on. _____ When you

feel your heart is pound-in', fear a dev-il's at your door,

there's no place to hide, you're fro-zen to the floor, what you

196

years, what you do then is you tell your-self to wait it out. You

say: It's this day, not me, that's bound to go a-

way. Child, hold on, it's this day, not you, that's

bound to go a - way.

A TRIP TO THE LIBRARY
from *She Loves Me*

Lyrics by SHELDON HARNICK
Music by JERRY BOCK

MISS RITTER: *(Spoken before the introduction) Let me tell you, you've never seen anything like that library. So many books. . . so much marble. . . so quiet!*

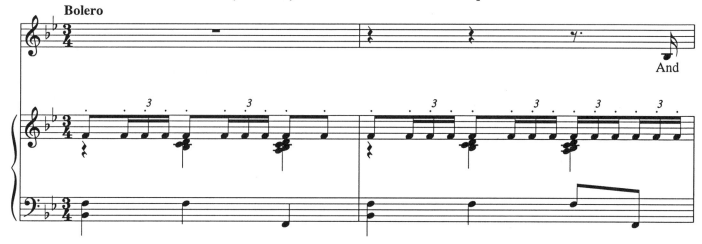

And

sud-den-ly all of my con-fi-dence drib-bled a-way with a pit-i-ful plop. My

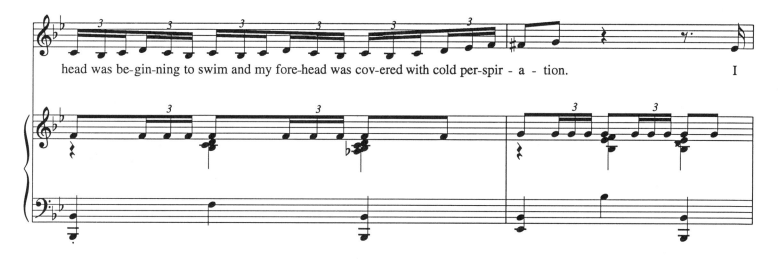

head was be-gin-ning to swim and my fore-head was cov-ered with cold per-spir - a - tion. I

start-ed to reach for a book and my hand aut-o-mat-i-c'lly came to a stop.

I

don't know how long I stood fro-zen, a vic-tim of pan-ic and mor-ti - fi - ca - tion.

With Freedom

Oh, _____ how I want-ed to flee _____ when a kind - ly voice, a

rall.   **Moderato**

gen - tle voice whis-pered "Par-don me."

And there _ was this dear, sweet, clear-ly re - spec - ta - ble thick-ly be - spec - ta - cled

man who stood _ by my side and qui - et - ly said _ to me "Ma'am,

Don't mean _ to in - trude, but I was just won - der-ing are you in need _ of some

help?" I said "no . . . Yes, I am!"

mf (*mf*)

The next thing I know I'm sip-ping hot choc-'late and tell-ing my trou-bles to Paul, whose ten-der brown eyes kept send-ing com-pass-ion-ate looks. A trip to the li-bra-ry has made a new girl of me, for sud-den-ly I can see the ma-gic of

books.   I

have to ad-mit in the back of my mind, I was pray-ing he would-n't get fresh.   And

all of the while I was won-der-ing why an il - lit - er - ate girl should at - tract   him.   Then

all of a sud-den he said that I could-n't go wrong with "The Way of All Flesh."   Of

course, it's a nov-el, but I did-n't know or I cer-tain-ly would-n't have smacked him. _____ Well, he gave me a

smile, _____ that I could-n't re - sist, _____ and I knew at once how

rall. **Moderato**

much I liked this op - tom - e - trist.

You know_ what this dear, sweet, slight-ly be - spec - tac-led gen-tle-man said _ to me

next? He said __ he could solve this prob-lem of mine. __ I said "How?"

He said __ if I'd like he'd will-ing-ly read __ to me some of his fav - or - ite

things. I said "When?" He said "Now." His nov - el ap -

proach seemed high-ly sus-pi - cious and pos-si - bly dan - ger-ous too. I told __ my-self

206

TELL ME ON A SUNDAY
from *Song and Dance*

Lyrics by DON BLACK
Music by ANDREW LLOYD WEBBER

Slowly

EMMA:

Don't write a let - ter when you want to leave.

Don't call me at 3 A. M. from a friend's a - part - ment. I'd

like to choose ___ how I hear the news. Take me to a park that's

210

EVERYBODY LOVES LOUIS

from *Sunday in the Park with George*

Music and Lyrics by
STEPHEN SONDHEIM

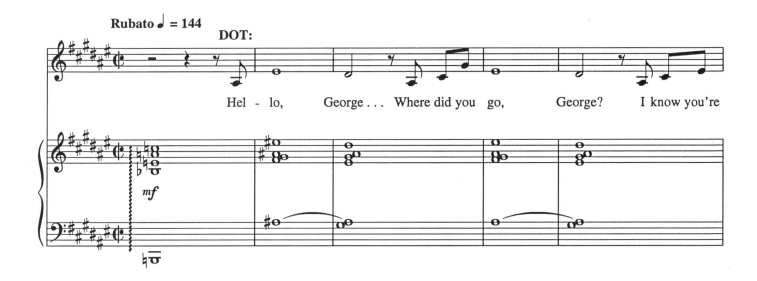

Hel - lo, George . . . Where did you go, George? I know you're

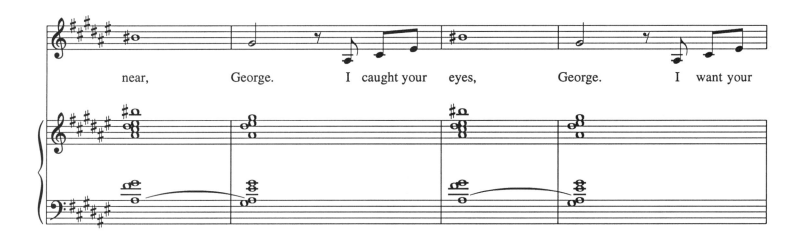

near, George. I caught your eyes, George. I want your

ear, George. I've a sur - prise,

lo, _____ George . . . _____

Lou - is' al - ways so pleas - ant,

Lou - is' al - ways so fair. Lou - is makes_ you feel pres - ent,

Lou - is' gen - er - ous. That's the thing_ a - bout Lou - is:

Lou - is al - ways is "there". Lou - is' thoughts are not

hard to fol - low, Lou - is' art is not hard to swal - low.

Not that Lou - is' per - fec - tion — That's what makes him i -

deal. Hard - ly an - y - thing worth ob - jec - tion:

220

Ev - 'ry - bod - y gets a - long_ with him. That's the trou - ble, noth - ing's wrong_ with him.

Lou - is has_ to bake his way, George can on - ly bake his . . .

(She licks a pastry)*

Lou-is it is!

*Actually, in the New York production, Dot stuffed her mouth with bread here, saying the last line with her mouth full.

IF HE REALLY KNEW ME

from *They're Playing Our Song*

Words by CAROLE BAYER SAGER
Music by MARVIN HAMLISCH